MW01625640
Primary
ZOO

For all those who, through their loving example, have taught me to strive to be my best self

—Candas M. Elder

For my own family zoo, reminding them that even silly monkeys can be reverent at church.

—Rocky Davies

Cover and interior design by Michelle Fryer

Published by Covenant Communications, Inc.
American Fork, Utah

Printed in China
First Printing: September 2018

22 21 20 19 18   10 9 8 7 6 5 4 3 2 1

ISBN: 978-1-52440-730-8

Lions and Tigers at Church, Oh My!

Written by Candas M. Elder
Illustrated by Rocky Davies

At Primary we find what is good and is true,
But sometimes on Sundays it feels like a ZOO!

In the halls children scurry, picking up speed,
Then burst through the doors in a **frenzied stampede.**

The teachers are ready with crayons in cases.
Happily greeting the righteous young faces.

"Welcome back!" Sister Kimberly says with a smile.
"We're excited to see you all here for a while.

Today we will learn of the love of the Savior
And how we should show Him our finest behavior."

The prayer is then offered by a **talkative ox**,
Who's grateful for all—including his socks.

Kangaroo hops up to deliver the scripture.
He reads about Noah and holds up a picture.

Ostrich is nervous about giving her talk.
When she opens her mouth all that's heard is a **squawk**.

The teacher says softly, "You're doing okay.
The Spirit," she tells her, "Helps us know what to say."

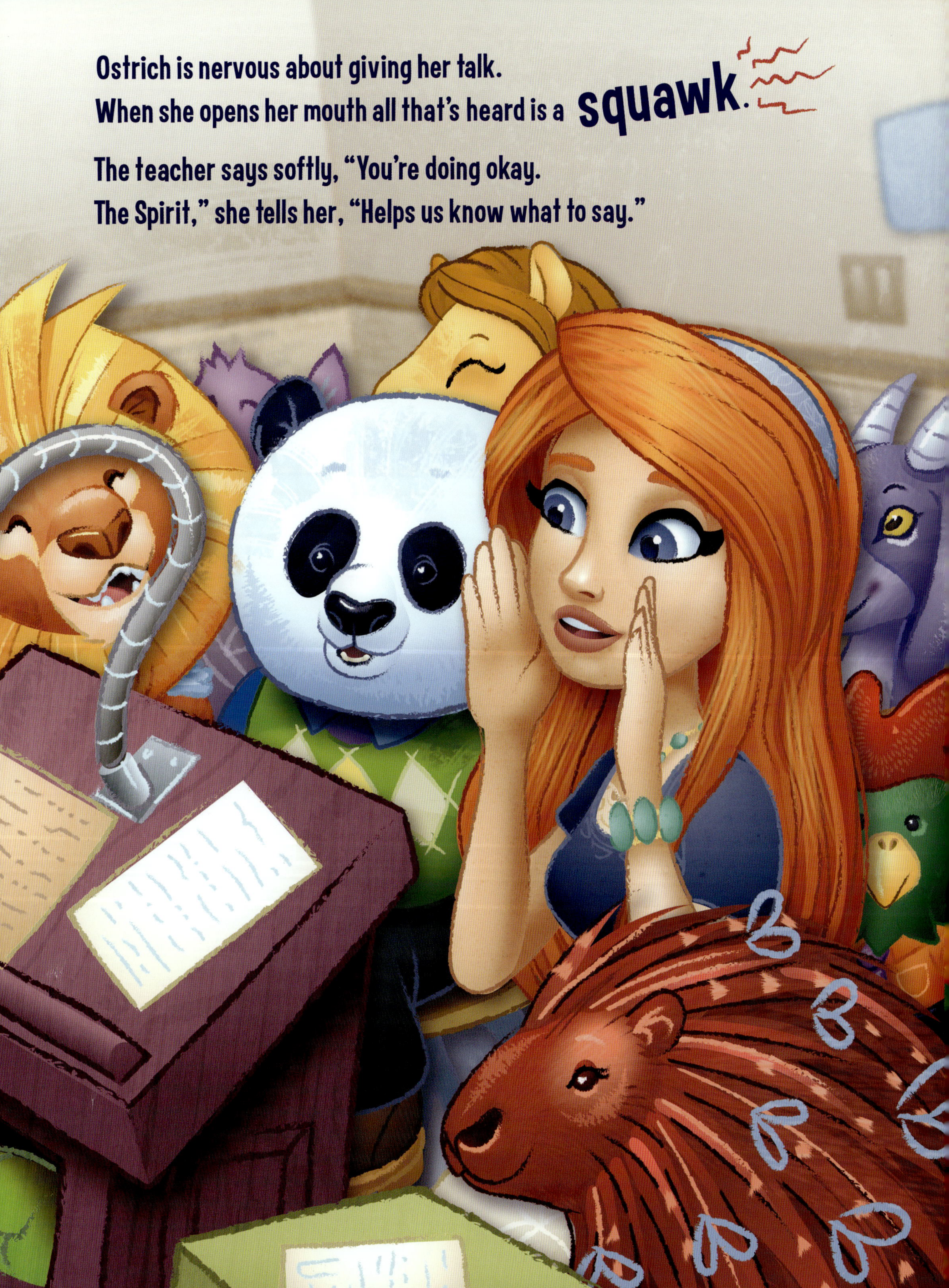

From the back of the room comes a **rambunctious cry**
From a penguin who's tangled all up in his tie.

And out of her seat comes the **thirstiest otter**,
Who's slid up to ask for her fifth drink of water.

Then **Fox waves** his paw for what seems like forever.
He knows all the answers because he's so clever.

The teacher asks them to please **take a seat.**
"Let's try to be reverent with our hands and our feet."

"Jesus adores every child, every creature.
He is our friend, Savior, Master, and Teacher."

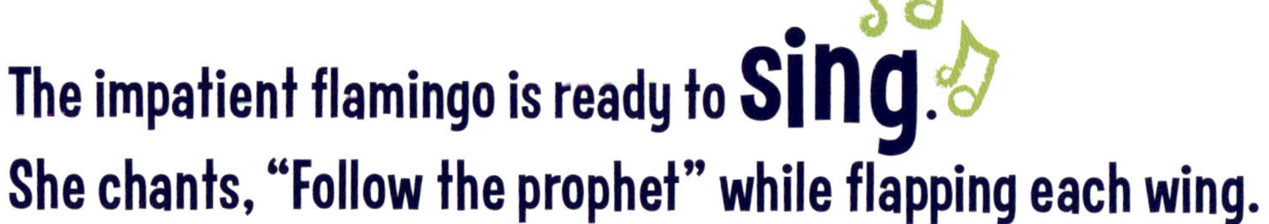

The impatient flamingo is ready to **sing**.
She chants, "Follow the prophet" while flapping each wing.

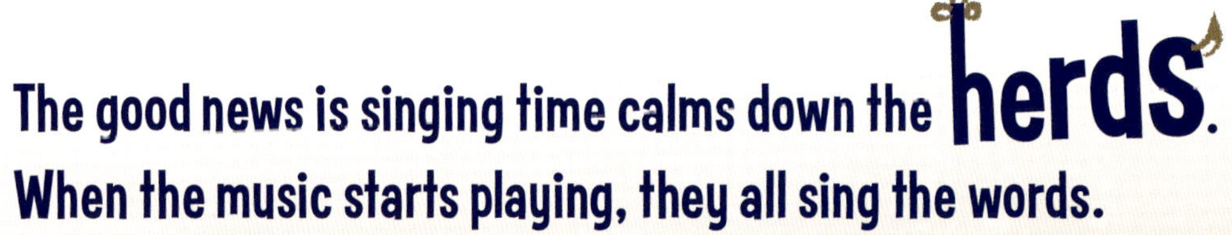
The good news is singing time calms down the herds.
When the music starts playing, they all sing the words.

Then, reverent at last, they all fold their hands,
And Giraffe gives a prayer up at the stand.

When the "amen" is said, they **head out the door**,
Until they come back next Sunday for more . . .

Because even though Primary can feel like a ZOO,
It's a place where the Spirit can teach what is true.

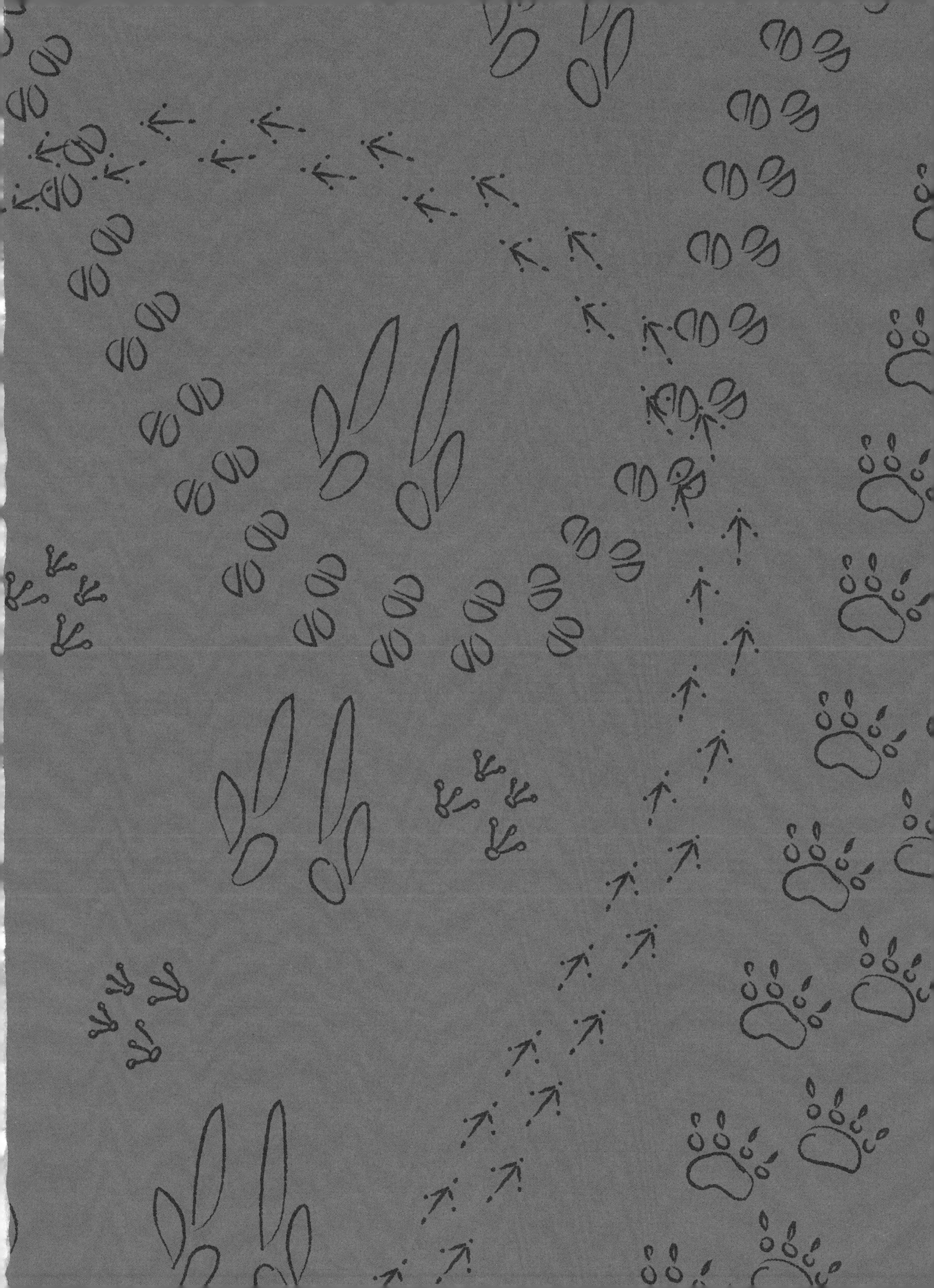